Unlocked
Chamber
of
Emotions

Joaly Picart
& Eric Harper Jr

Order this book online at www.trafford.com
or email orders@trafford.com

Most Trafford titles are also available at major online book retailers.

Printed in the United States of America.

ISBN: 978-1-4669-7096-0 (sc)
ISBN: 978-1-4669-7095-3 (e)

Trafford rev. 01/03/2013

 www.trafford.com

North America & international
toll-free: 1 888 232 4444 (USA & Canada)
phone: 250 383 6864 ♦ fax: 812 355 4082

Contents

Sad Poems

Angry Poems

Low Self Esteem

Random

Romantic

Sad Poems

My heart is done
(Joaly)

Seven times my heart had been broken
Broken into pieces
There was only a little piece of it
And
You took it
You took the last piece
And
Didn't handle it with care
Now it is all broke all gone
All gone
My heart is gone
I am sitting here with no heart
No heart
I don't know what to do
I had been crying
I had been crying
I had crying myself to sleep
I had been crying all day and night
I have no heart
I had been crying
I had been sitting in this cold world
All alone

The world is so cold
So cold . . .
And dark . . .
So dark . . . And black
So black . . .
There no red . . .
No red . . .
Oh red where are u? . . .
I am siting here crying and hoping one day I will find red . . .
My heart is done
People had been walking all over it
Now I don't have no heart
Because
It is all gone
All done
So done . . .
So done . . .
Done

Over Over Again
(Joaly)

Every day and night . . . .
I had been thinking of you . . . Baby . . .
I don't know what to do without you . . .
Oh . . . .
Every night I had been thinking of you . . . .
I had been crying for you to come back to me
I miss you so much that it makes me want to cry
Over . . . over . . . over
I had been wondering
If you are still mine
If you heart is still mine
If you still love me
Over . . . over . . . . over again
I had been thinking of you . . . .
Over . . . over . . . over . . .
I can? t image you with another woman
Over . . . . over . . . . over again . . .
I had been crying . . . crying . . . crying . . . .
I know now and had learn my lesson
I won't lie to you again
Baby? . . .
I love you . . . . so much . . . .
That I dream about you every single day and night
I can't take you off of my mind
Baby . . . .

Freezer
(Joaly)

I miss you like crazy.
I got tears in my eyes.
Im loosing my baby.
Why baby why?
I am a lost soul,
If I can't have you.
Lord please help me.
Tell me what to do.
Will you come back to me?
Your soul is fading fast.
Don't be gone forever,
Without you I won't last.
My body aches,
As my tears soak the sheets.
My cries are drowned in silence,
I've been heart broken for weeks.
It's a cold cold world,
Come back and wipe my tears.
Sweep me off my feet,
Baby take me out of hear.

Do You remember the girl
(Joaly)

Do you remember the girl the girl you used?
Do you remember the girl that you used to beat?
Do you remember the girl you lied to?
Do you remember the girl?
Do you remember the girl that you might had cheated on?
Do you remember the girl?
Do you remember her?
Do you remember the girl that spoil you so much that even when you
    didn't deserve it?
Do you remember her?
Do you remember the girl that dare your frist child?
Do you remember her?
Do you remember that girl?
Sometime she wonder?
If you realy did love her?
If you ment everything that you say to her?
If you really wanted to married her?
Sometime she wonder
If you ever think about your daughter?
Do you ever wonder how is she doing?
Do you ever wonder if she look like you?
Do you ever wonder if she is in good hands?
Do you even every worry about your little girl?

Darkness
(Joaly)

Oh Yes
I was once in a very dark place in my life
I was so sad, lonely, and miserable
I couldn't think strait
I felt like life couldn't go one
People walked all over me
I been through hell and back
I was so depress
After I fell off track
All I wanted is
For someone to respect me
Listen to me
And love me for who I am
I was living in a downward spiral
Being in relationships with the wrong dudes
I was in two abusive relationship
End up having a baby by one
I wanted to give up on life
Until I fell in love with a awesome dude
My life got better from thereafter
I hope this path continues

Taking My Hope up

Sometime
I wonder why you don't like me back
I realy do like you
I know I did it again
Took my hope up
Mush my own heart
I did it all on my own
You didn't do anything
You didn't me any pain
SO I will be alright
I am the one who fall for you
You didn't
None of this is your fault
It is mine
Please don't waste your trying to apology
For the pain I am in
So sweetie stops feeling sorry for me
Stop feeling guilty
Just answer few questions for me
Then I will leave you alone
I want honest answers
What made you not like me
Am I too ugly?
I not sexy?
Not smart an enough
not funny enough?

Seven Times My heart had been broken

My heart has been reduced to pieces.
I've manage to salvage some
After you destroyed what was left,
Now I have none
You took those pieces,
Now there is nothing there
You mishandled my heart,
With no compassion and lack of care

I don't know what to do
I had been crying
I had been crying myself to sleep
I had been crying all day and night
I have no heart
I had been crying
I had been sitting in this dark cold world
All alone

Where is our Friendship?

We grew up together
We knew each other for a very long time
We knew each other family member
We knew each other lifetime
We knew each other well
But
I never understand this
Why did you tell your friends you didn't know me?
Why did you ignore me when I tired to talk to you?
Why did you treat me like a stranger?
Why did you do this all to me?
After all those years
We knew each other
We are supposed to be best friend
We are supposed to be cool as a cat
We are supposed to be like family
I want to know why
Is it something I did?
Or
Is it something that you didn't like about me
Or is it something my friends did to you
Tell me

Because I want to know
So I can clean this all up
I want to clean this misunderstanding
I want to clean all this hatred in between us
I want to start all over
If It is because I gave you too much drama
Then I am sorry for that
And
I meant it
I am sorry
If it is something that my friends did
Then I am sorry for what they did
If it is something I did
Well I am sorry

Love was not an Enough
(Joaly)

Love was not an enough to keep
You from abusing me
Love was not an enough to keep
You from raping me
Love was not an enough to keep
You from lying to me
Love was not an enough to keep
You from cheating on me
Love was not an enough to make
You see me that <u>I loved you from all of My Heart</u>
I guess <u>Love never an Enough</u>

How can you say that You "love" me?
(Joaly)

How can you say you "love" me?
When you don't respect me
How can you say you "love" me?
When you lie to me so many times
How can you say you "love" me?
When you keep cheating on me
How can you say you "love" me?
When you keep abusing me
How can you say you "love" me?
When you can't even accept me for who I am
How can you????

Frustrated with Love
(Joaly)

I love you with all of my heart
But that was not an enough to keep you
I love you with all of my soul
But that was still not an enough to stop you from leaving
I love you with all of my spirit
But that was not an enough again to stop you from lying
I love you with all of my body part
But that still again was not an enough to keep you from wanting her
I gave up on loving you

Done with Life

I can't continue to live
In a world that's cold and twisted
I can't continue to love
When boys continue to take my heart and rip it
I don't want to keep on making friends
If people are going to be two faces
I rather be along then to be with all the disgraces,

Where are you

When will you come and carry me home
When will you put your arm around me
When will you
Make me all your
I am so tired of being sick tired of having pain
Nobody can fix me
Oh . . . no . . . oh . . . no . . . oh . . . no
Nobody can find out what is wrong with me
I had been in pain every night
My stomach hurt
My head hurt
My heart hurt
I don't know why
I need you
Come home to me

In and out of Life
(Joaly)

In and out of life
Is how people will go.
There is no hope
For people to grow
Old with you because
In and out of life
That is how people will go
Sometimes once or twice.
In and out of life
Like a revolving door
People come and people go
While the heart grows sore.
Settling down sounds
Like a song from the 80s.
In and out of relationships,
Making bastard babies.
It's crazy but
It's the reality we live in.
10 thousand followers who Liked
You call your friends.
Social circles
Come a dime a dozen.
If you don't believe me,
Ask your neighbor's landlord's mailman cousin.

Done with Love

Can't you see I am hurt?
Can't you see my heart?
Can't take it any more
I am so Hurt
I don't know what to do
I thought that I had found love
But why you have to do it to me
I guess I was wrong
And I will never find my true love
Because every time I thought that I had found love
I always end up losing it
I am tired of searching for love
I don't know why I have trouble finding love
When I know I am a beautiful girl
With a beautiful heart
Why nobody want a beautiful girl with beautiful heart?
Don't she deserve to be love?

Angry Poems

Leave my Life Alone
(Remix Eric)

Do you know how much I loathe you? Do you know that I hate you?
Don't you know that we will never be friends? I don't want to talk to
  you
ever again. I refuse to be in your presence, peasant. Not even if we had
  to. I'm
though with you.
Don't buy me flowers you coward. Because whatever you give me won't
  stay.
Being with you is like a nightmare that never goes away. It will never
  happen
So, leave me alone!
Take your stupid gifts, your unwanting love and be gone. All of the
  second
chances I gave you are blown.

Player
(Joaly)

I don't want to be with you
I don't want to talk to you
I don't want to see you
Because you are a player
And you know that being a player hurt people feeling
But you still being one
And that make no senses
If you love your girlfriend, you didn't want to hurt her
And if you love your girlfriend, you could not have been a player
So that mean you are not a good boyfriend
So get away from me
Because
I don't want to have a boyfriend, who is a player like
You . . .
I had a feeling that we should end our relationship for good
Because I am tired of looking back at our relationship
And see how we fight
We had fight a lot
The fighting is making me tire of you
I am not trying to said that I am mad that you because our relationship
    was
not 100% perfect
24
I know that no relationship is 100% perfect
And I know no relation fights like our

I feel like I had been dating the wrong man for two whole years
So I think it is time for you to go
So give me my last kiss
My last hug
And give me a handshake and say
Goodbye . . .
Goodbye forever
Don't call me
Don't write to me
Don't come over
Because every time I see you or hear from you
I will ignore you,
Because
I will hate you forever and ever
Until
I lay down to
Die . . .

Fine whatever

If you are going to walk around saying that you don't know
Fine
If you are going to walk around and say that you are not dating me
Fine
If you going to try to avoid me in the public
But you are all over me when nobody is around
Fine whatever
I don't care no more
I don't need you

Fine Whatever
(remix by Eric)

You are going to walk around
You're not dating me
But when nobody is around
You are all over me
If you going to be my boyfriend
Then show me the respect that I deserve
Instead of breaking my heart
And getting on my last nerves
How you going to be my true love
When I don't want to have sex you force yourself onto me.
I wish I can have back what you took from me
My virginity

Lie Lies and even more Lies

Lies and more lies That is all you can do You lie from here to there You are the king of false truths.
I don't know why I ever dated you at all. You're a lying, filthy,
Cheating, deceitful dog.
When you came into my life,
You were the best thing I ever had.
You were suave, sexy, and skillful,
You got good at being bad.
You said I was your honey,
And you were my bee.
But I felt more like your door mat,
Because you walk all over me.
It's time to cut the cord,
But you were once my idol.
You turned into a whore,
Losing you is suicidal.
To you emotions are a game,
And you played it so well.
I felt like it would never be my turn,
It was like a living hell.
You say your family are practicing Christians,
Well they should practice a little harder.
You said that you are educated,
So I thought that you were smarter.

Player
(Remix Eric)

I'm tired of the tears,
And I'm tired of crying.
I'm tired of forgiving,
And I'm tired of trying.
You stabbed me in the back,
Yeah you're a bonfire traitor.
My love for you was great.
But my hatred for you is greater.
So do what you do best,
And walk out of the door.
Cause I don't want to be,
With a player no more.

I am not Jealous
(Joaly)

You played with my heart.
Told me rap and lies. But you never told me.
About the other girl on the side.
You just broke my heart into little pieces.
I had so much love for you kid. So much that,
I couldn't explain how much I did.
Your hurt me,
You made me cry.
You told me you loved me,
While staring at me eyes.
You discovered the formula for sugar,
By saying everything I wanted to hear.
But when the truth came out,
That sugar turned into tears.
You are nothing more to me,
Then a grain of sand.
Now that you are history,
I have a new man.
He loves me for who I am,
He is the man I want to be with.
You are my past, you're my cancer,
You made me dream, you made me sick.

"Are you done acting dumb?"
(Joaly)

yo girl
you need to calm your ass down
You think you are the "bomb"
ha ha oh Please!!! take a hike
You think you are better
Think again cause you are dreaming
You think you are prettier
Damn you are just jealous
You can't cook
You are lazy
You are two faced
You love to spread gossips
You are so spoil
You are the most spoil child that I ever met
You are the rudest person out that I ever know
And
You dare to turn around and tell me that you know how to "Act"
OH Please
Let me ask you something
Are you done acting dumb?

Gave back the Ring and Roll . . . .

You might have wonder why
I gave back the ring and roll
So I am going to tell you now
You better listen to me carefully
Here it goes
You knew that I love you
When we first met
You were all I was looking for
But
You were wearing a mask
You were not the one I fell in love with
You had two personalize
Slow
Time after time
Your mask came off
Your personally slowly came out
You became violet
You started lying to me
Abusing me
Telling me that You love me
But yet you didn't
You were wasting my time
So I gave back the ring and roll
I had tired my hardest
I had try to make you happy
Feel special
I was not successful in none of that
I tried to make love with you but
You push me away
Made a special valentine dinner
But your lies mess it up
So I threw my ring on the floor and walk out the door

Hey Chris
(Joaly)

Hey Chris
I gave you my heart, my soul and my blood
But for some reasons that was not an enough
I created a river crying over you
But yet you didn't seem to care
You continue to do your things
Lie, cheat, and yeah add abuse to the list
I stood by your side no matter what
Even when you did me wrong
Treat me like a child
Hit me with a belt
I scream for you to stop
But yet you didn't hear
What did I do to deserve this?
What did I do to deserve the abuse?
Why did you treat those ugly white water back like queen but me as shit?
I loved you with all of my heart
They didn't.
I guess you like to treat people who don't care for you good
And
People who love you evil
I guess karma already came after you

Get out of My face

You need to get out of my face
I can't stand you anymore
You made me sick to my stomach
Really want to throw up in Your face
All those lies and all those girls
You just made me sick
So you need to get out of my face
Before
I put you out in the hospital

Cut the Lame excuses and the Bullshit

I am so fucking sick of this crap
You know that I know
You are still in love with that girl
You know She ain't fro you
I am
But
Damn it
You are giving me divided love
Since, when I ever gave you division love?
So why are you doing this?
You want fucking privacy
What are you hiding
What is your secret
You know that You are wrong
And
I am right
So cut the lame excuses and the bullshit
Because
We both know that you ani't making no damn senses
You either
Give me all of your heart and love
Or
Go back with that
Fucking ugly young duck who has no class . . .

You and I together never
(Joaly)

You and I Together? no
why?
hide me from your family
keep the world from knowing that I am you
giving me nothing, no flowers, no gifts, never go on a date with me
that is fine with me
but come to me and expect me give you sex
never
not my style of relationship
so you and I together?
never not this life time not even the next

Yo Bitch

You need to fall the heck back
Find your own damn man
My man don't even want your nasty butt
So shoo fly
Go fly to a night club
Fuck someone in there and leave mine alone

Yo Bitch

Yo Bitch
Who do you think you are?
You need to shut your mouth up
Cause nothing really come out of your mouth but garbage
No wonder your breath be kicking
But let me tell you young duck something
You need to keep my name out your landfill
Before I give you something to dump in your landfill

The Loser can have it all

The loser can have it all
He can take whatever he wants
I don't really care
Because
I just want him out of my life
So you loser pack your bag
Take whatever you want
And
Never ever come back

"Coward"
(Joaly)

You raped me
Let you said you didn't
Then you want me to forgive you
But you can't even ambit that you did what did
You can't even say you are sorry
Yet you want me to forgive you
Loll really You lost your damn mind
You must be dreaming
You coward I am ani't going to forgive you

What is your problem little dude?

What is your problem dude?
why you always give me an attitude?
why always calling me names?
why you always like to see me mad and hurt?
You can have an attitude
but
You can can't give me an attitude
why?
Because, I already have one
so
you better not start with me
name calling
that is what you like to do
Huh?
I had been called by different names from all of my life
so you can call me whatever you want
but You can't call me a hoe
You know what?
I think that you are jealous
because
I got a man
and I bet that you like me
but
someone who is a punk like you
can't express their feelings
and that is shame
Thanks God that I am not dating you

If I did
could be done with you
because
I am here for you
I know that I can't change things
but
I can gab able make you happy for once
so . . .
You better start letting out your feelings . . . .
I notice that you love to
make me mad
pick on me
call me names
but why? . . . . Do you like me or something?
do you want me?
What is your problem little dude?
why are you hiding?
Just tell me
what is your problem little dude?

Low Self Esteem

If . . .

If it was not for me to be deaf
I won't be living this horrible life
If it was not for me to be deaf
Maybe everybody won't be hating me so much
If I was not for me to be deaf
Guy won't be cheating on me
If it was not for me to be deaf
Maybe I won't had be in an abuse relationship
If it was not for me to be deaf
I could be my parent's favorite child
if it was not for me to be deaf
I could of be love
If it was not for me to be deaf . . . .

Why me

Sometime
I wonder why me?
Why do I have to go through abuse?
Why do I have to go through rape?
What did I do?
What did I do to deserve all this?
Can't you see me crying?
Crying for you to stop
Why you like hurting me?
Why you like to see me cry?
Why do you like breaking my heart?
Don't you know that I love you with all of my heart?
Tell me . . .
What did I do?
What did I do to deserve all this?

Random

Imperfection
(Joaly)

If you want to somebody perfect
Well . . .
Then it seen to be
Good bye . . .
Good bye and Good luck
Good luck with finding
A perfect girlfriend
I just want to let you know that
Nobody is perfect
Not even singers
Not writer
Not even famous people
And not even you
Not even you . . .
So Good Luck
Being perfect is boring
Didn't you tired yourself being perfect
I guess not
If you did
You will be bore yourself
You will have a very few friends
Nobody wants to be perfect
Everybody have something wrong with wrong
You have something wrong with you too . . .

Heart problems
Walking problems
Blacking problems
Learning problem
Talking problems
Hearing problems
No Bobbies are perfect
People make mistakes
Why can't you just
Accept the mistake, learn from it and move on
I told 100 times before
That nobody is perfect
I am getting really tire of telling you
If you do not believe me
I guess that I will leave it up to you
Why can't you just accept?
Your girlfriend's personally
And if she is 100 % perfect

Imperfection
(remix by Eric)

Perfection's a misconception,
But we're always looking for it in a mate.
We look for qualities that isn't reality,
Which is why it's hard to find a date.
Wanting specific characteristics,
Curves in the right places.
Stereotypical features,
Ethnic grooves on their faces.
We must learn how to accept,
Each other's imperfections.
Or our narrow mindedness,
Will make a bad first impression.

N is not My name
(joaly)

One day I was walking down the street
And pass group white boys
Then I saw a black boy walked pass them
One of white boys said? What up nigger?
The black boy just walked by
The white boy shouted that the black boy? Hey nigger don't be scared
    of us.
We won't hurt you. Do you think you can breathe us? If you think so
    then you
are wrong because you are nothing but a big fat nigger?
The black boy just kept on walking and never looked back
And from that day on
I wondered why people look at the color of people's skins
Color of people's skin don't make any different but only their personality
If you want to have friends
Look at their personality and not their skins,
And show them respect

N that is not my Name
(remix by Eric)

Was it real,
Or just my imagination.
I was walking down the street,
When I witnessed a confrontation.
White boy shoulder bumped,
He must of been in a rush I figure.
My mind changed as he sounded,
Watch where you going Nigger.
Shockwaves went through my body,
When that N word hit my ear.
But the black boy kept on walking,
As if he didn't hear.
The next day, I ask the black boy,
Why wasn't he offended.
He said when he looked at his birth certificate,
Nigger wasn't in it

Child to Adult

Now
That I am adult
My learning will never stop
My mistakes will never stop either
I will continue to fall and I will get boos on my knee or shoulder
But
I can't go crying to my mommy or daddy to make my boos all better
Because
Now that I am adult
I have to face the world and challenge all on my own
I know that there will be time
When
I wish I was a young once again
having a mommy or daddy face the world for me is do much easier
I can't wish that
I know that facing the world/ challenge is the only way I will learn

Child to Adult
(remix by Eric)

Although I am an adult
My learning will never stop
My mistakes will never stop either
I will continue to fall
And I will get bruises on my body but
I can't go crying to my parents to make my scars all disappear
Because now that I am an adult
I have to conquer my challenges all on my own
I know that there will be time when
I wish I was young once again
Having parents to fight my battles and face my fears
I know that's unrealistic
Because only I can cry my cries, regardless who wipe my tears.

A False Man

A false man don't need to be here in this world
Cause false men ani't doing no good in this world
Leaving you asking yourself when will we have a world full of real men
What is a false man?
A false man is a guy who
Rape people
Lie and cheat
Abuse people
Is a gang member and kills
Do drugs/drinks (all the time)
Don't have a good head on it shoulder
Also a false man tell a woman that "he loves will never hurt her lie to her
    always be there for her when she need him

No Justice—Just Us
(Joaly)

Everyday
As I wake up
I say a little prayer to my heavenly father
to protect me in every move I make
because
Judging the color of skin I am in
I don't feel like I am safe anywhere
I could have my life taken in the next few hours
by a someone who doesn't like the skin I'm wearing
They could kill me because I look harmful with my hoodie on
Walking down the block minding my own business
even though
I never committed a crime in my life
I will still lose the case
they will win
I will end up with no justice
all because
The COLOR OF MY SKIN

Falsity

By Eric K. Harper Jr.

We watch reality TV
And we live on the web,
Real life has become scripted.
Accountability is dead.
We wonder if there's a God,
Have you any shame?
We worship Mark, Noah, and Thomas,
Cause websites bear their name.
Courtship on the internet,
Is engaging yet bereft.
I have stain the blogosphere with my heart and spirit,
It's as if I never left.

I Have A Dream Too

By Eric K. Harper Jr.

I wonder if it is really alive.
Haunted by discrimination and racism at the polls.
Amnesty is a dish best serve cold.
Victories are won at the price of lives that are lost.
Equality seems to have never been discovered.
And it may never will.
Dependence has become taboo.
Relinquished of our benevolence.
Economic greed is evident.
Although we love to hate and hate to love,
MLK dream shall still live on.

Faith

By Eric K. Harper Jr.

He who has sight takes for granted
As far as the eyes can see.
He who has blindness
Only has faith that leads.
He who is deaf
Listens with his heart.
While he who is hearing
Stays lost in the dark.
Sometimes our senses
Can lead us into the abyss.
We must learn to turn to faith.
We can start by doing this: -_-

Uncounted vote

By Eric K. Harper Jr.

Interpretation without education leads to anarchy.
The Constitution of confusion was ratified by oligarchy.
Casting votes at the polls is preface by doubt and hesitation.
Since the poor are enslaved by taxation without representation.

Color Blind
(Eric)

A declaration of color blindness,
Is a declaration of ignorance,
A denial of inheritance:
Centuries of injustice.

Racism is a fungus,
That grows inside of our hearts.
In dark spaces where only hate is,
That is where it starts.

If you are color blind,
Then you should wear your color glasses,
So your eyes can witness,
Just how beautiful being black is.

Romantic

"Meaning of true love"

I hate marriage today
because
not a lot of people married each other for love
some people married the person
because . . .
they are tired of looking for love
some people married the person married
because of what
they like what see on the other person body
some people married a person
because
the other person makes more money than they do
but
very few marry
because of
'Love'
I hate love today
because
nobody understand the
true meaning of love
oh love
where are you
I had been opening doors
All I had found was
Boys playing basketball
and
Dogs darkling because the meal was good
but
no boyfriend of mine
no guys for me
no love . . . .

I was so tire
I was so heartbroken
So I gave up on searching for love
I sat down on my poach set looking up in the sky
and tears started to come out of my eyes
and didn't stop until there was a river of tears
I had cry a river
because
I couldn't find my true love
As
I continue to cry a river
A Man came to me
And
Sat down next to me
wrapped my tears up
and
Asked me why I cried a river
As I was telling him
I felt his hand around me
I felt warm being there
As
WE contain to talk
I knew that my true love had finally came
I looked up in the sky and Smile
the sun came out and dried out my river
and
left a rainbow
oh love . . . .
oh love . . .
oh love . . . .

I will see again soon
(Joaly)

I know this is early
but
my heart say you are the one
You make me feel like I am young and in love
we hold hands and kiss the entire time
You make my world seem so much better
I know this way to early
But I got to let it out
I think I am falling in love with you
because
I found myself thinking of you countless
I find myself reaching for you when I am sleeping but finding you not
    there make me kind of sad but I tell myself I will see you again soon

You Complete me
(Eric)

I don't mean to be too bold and forward but,
My heart say you are the one.
When we hold hands and kiss,
I feel so in love and so young.

You complete my world,
That is no doubt.
These feelings I have inside,
I got to let them out.

Allow me to keep it real,
I always see you in my dreams.
You're like a film strip on a reel,
Now hush this is my favorite scene.

You are the one
(Joaly)

My heart says you are the one
My mind say to take it slow
My heart is saying yes
But my mind is telling me no
My heart is racing
My mind is saying slow down
I'm like a tree when you're not around
My branches break and I sigh a sad sound
You know how I feel
And you know I'm not lying
Pore your feelings on paper
And stop my heart from crying

You are on my mind
(Joaly)

From dusk till dawn
You are on my mind
I think about you
All the time
Every time I am around you
I get butterflies
I Love you
I learned what love is
The day I met you
If you propose to me right now
I grantee I'll say I do

Do you feel the Same
(Joaly)

I miss you
I still Love you
Sometime I wonder
If you feel the same
Do you miss me?
Do you still love me?
Do you think about me sometime
Because I do
Since we broke up
Things had not been the same without you
I had been crying for you
I had been thinking about you
And
I had been wondering
If you feel the same
I can't stand the fact that we are over for good
Because we were supposed to be together forever
We fight a lot
We gave up onto each other
But
The truth is
I still Love you
I sometime I wonder
If you feel the same . . . .

You are the reason
(Joaly)

You are the reason why I believe in love at the first sight
my heart beat
Every day and night
Because of you
You caught me watch romantic movies
And in fairy tales
You brought the best out of me
You are the reason why
I am able to deal with this stupid world
You are the reason why . . .

I love it
(Joaly)

I love the way he make me feel
I love it
I love the way he kiss me
I love it
I love the way he make love to me
I love it
I love the way his dark smooth chocolate body relax against my smooth vanilla
body
I love it
I love the way how our eyes talk to one another
I love it
I love the way how his smile make me smile
His laugh make me laugh
I love it
I love the way how he makes my heart beat for him
I love it
I love the way he makes me feel when I cuddle with him
My heart is his only his
Nobody will ever make me stop loving him
No matter what happen between us
I will always love you

True Love

By Eric K. Harper, Jr.
Love is beautiful,
Like a sun that set.
Cherish it dearly,
Like the day you first met.
Love is respect,
Caring and trust.
A spiritual and physical,
Bond is a must.
True love is rare,
So never let it go.
Once you acquire it,
Give it a chance to grow.

Loving you
(Joaly)

Loving you is like running in a race
And I just can't compete
No matter how hard I love
My heart is champion in defeat

The gun fires
And there off
But the same day I found love
Was the same day love was lost

Well I made it to the finish line
And I made first place
Where hearts heal and loves a steal
I am happy I ran a good race

Him and me

His smooth chocolate body
And my dark vanilla body
Make the perfect candy in the entire world
When we put our body together
It don't fight over who is better
The two of us
Smoothing each other body
Slow make love
Our lips touch each other
Slow
We being to work on each other body like blender
And take turn burn up the room
But
Never let each other burn
Slow
We link each other until we hit the spot
Screaming each other name
Whispering in each other ear
Sucking on each other neck
Letting our body tell each other that we love each other and we ment to
  be together

Boyfriend
(Joaly)

A boyfriend can be a friend
A boyfriend can make you feel special
A boyfriend can make you go crazy
A boyfriend can have a good shoulder to cry or sleep on
A boyfriend is a person who you share your feeling with
A boyfriend can feel like he was your son
Because you share your love
You make sure he has everything that he need
You feed him and
You care for him

The first Time

The first time we met
I fell in love with you
You took all of my attention
I couldn't take my eye off of you
At night I dream about you
You are so handsome
Every day when I see you
All what I want to do is
Hug and kiss you
I want to hold your hands
Every time I try to said hi to you
My body just freeze
Oh
I can't stop thinking about you
You took all of my attention
When I am around you
You make me feel
Warm and cozy
I don't know how I fell in love with you
I just did
The first time we met
Was a beautiful moment of my life . . .

Silly

My name shine

I can't wait until My name is shinning
Shinning so bright
Everywhere I go
People will be shoring my name
Everybody will be calling me
My name will be so shiny
My picture will be everywhere
Because
I will be a star
I will be the Princess of America
Because
I am so wonderful
I am so beautiful
Oh. Oh . . .
I can't wait
I just can't wait
I can't wait for people to call me and ask me for help
I can't wait my name to be so bright
I will be everywhere
Because
I am wonderful
I am beautiful
I can't wait until my name be shining

Jail House

Damn
It is like prison in here
They will give you punishment
Everything you do that they don't like
You have to dress like an old lady
Or
You will get suspend
You have to act like You are in the military
Or dentition is where you will go
They will waste your time
Teaching you thing that really don't matter
Like trash land
Who want to learn about that crap?
I am soon graduate
I am so sure that I will never come back to visit
Because
I am sure I will get dentin
For hugging a teacher after a long time no seem
But
Thanks God
I only have a few months left then
I will be finally free at least . . . .

Mr. Grouchy

Oh Mr. Grouchy
Why are you always grouchy
Why are you always mad
Why you always have an attitude
Oh Mr. Grouchy . . . Mr. Grouchy
Is your father Oscar the Grouch?
Always grouchy
Always mean
Always having an attitude
Never satisfy with anything
Mr. Grochy Mr. Grouchy
Why your face always burning with anger
What is so good about being grouchy?
You are so grouchy that I swear you will be making Grouchy babies
I feel bad for them babies

New York Vs. Philly

New York suck
New York smell like poop poo
New York is stupid as a fuck
Philly is the shit
Philly is the World
Philly rock the world
Go Philly . . . Go Philly . . . Go Philly
It is your birthday
Party like it is your birthday
Kick it like it is your birthday
We will be Jamming like it is your birthday
We will be pooping like it is your birthday
Go Philly . . . Go Philly . . . Go Philly . . .
New York can kiss my ass . . . .

Christian

God

King of Love and peace
Watch over us days and nights
Safe us from evils
Listen to us
Love us no matter what
Help us though hard time
Speak to us though bible or send other people to talk to us for him
Send his only beloved some
Though virgin woman
Name Mary
So that Jesus could die
On the Cross
For Our Solvation
And when we done with our time on earth
We will go with him.

"Because the Lord was with me!"

My life
I look back and
I said to myself
wow I came a long way
used to sleep on the street
Hardy ate anything
hardy could take a shower
but
one day I woke up in an warm cozy bed and a clean blanket keeping me
    warm . . .
I had survive because . . .
the Lord was with me . . .
Lord was with me
from this day I have the Lord by my side and
because of that
I could do anything
I could be anything that I want to be
because the Lord is with me
the Lord is my savoy
Lord watch over me every day and night

the lord is the one who one who gave the strength to do the things I need
    to do
I could do anything with him on my side . . .
I became successful and living a good life
because
the Lord was with me.
Darkness Time
oh yes
I was once in the darkness life time
I was down
I was sad
I was lonely
I was miserable

Because the Lord was with me
(remix)

My life
I look back and said to myself
Wow I came a very long way
I used to sleep on the street
Hardy ate anything
Because the lord was with me
I could do anything
So I pray to Lord to help me get though
And guess what he did
He helps me
He helps me get though
Because the Lord was with me
With him I could anything
I asked the Lord to help me with my book
And my book was published
Because the lord was with me
Jesus was with me
I was having trouble with finding a play to stay after my time was up at
    the shelter
I pray to God to help me find a place
A few days later I got a phone call saying they have a place believe for
    me to rent
Because the Lord was with me
Because God was with me
I could do anything
Hauhja
Praise to the Lord
Because the Lord was with me

"When I was little"

when I was little I used to wonder
who made the earth, the sky, the birds and the animals?
who create nights, days and everything's else?
one day my mom got me to Sunday school
I learn God made the
Earth, the sky, the birds and the animals, days, nights and everything's else
I got on my knee and give thanks to the Lord for all of his hard work
from this day on I worship the Lord your Jesus

Holiday

Mother Day
(by Joaly)

Mother's day,
It is a special date.
It's a time to show,
How much we appreciate.
Our mothers,
And all the hard work that they've done.
They deserve two holidays,
Instead of only one.
If I may say,
Giving flours is cliché.
I would rather write a poem,
Here's what I have to say.
Roses are dead.
Violets are too.
Happy Mother's day,
Mom I love you.

Mother Day
(Remix by Eric)

Mother's day is a time
We sent time with our lovely mother like you
We buy our mother roses to show that
We love her
We make our mom dinner show her that
We care about her
We give our mom a huge to show her that
We will always be there for her
Even though we are growing and soon are living on
Our own